Date: 3/15/12

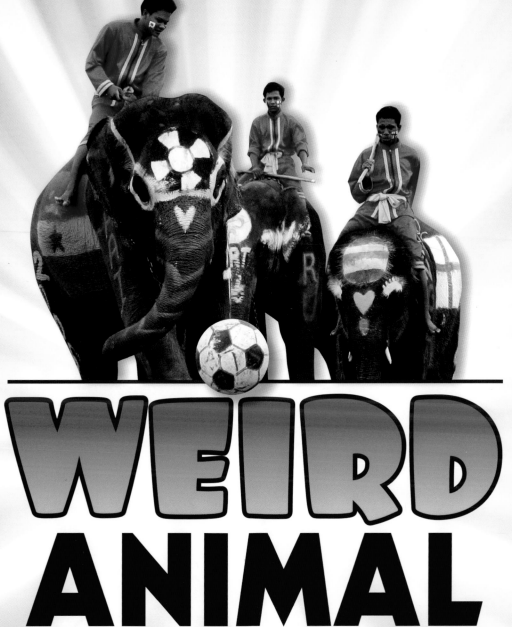

WEIRD
ANIMAL SPORTS

By S.B. Watson

The Child's World®

Published by The Child's World®
1980 Lookout Drive
Mankato, MN 56003-1705
800-599-READ
www.childsworld.com

The Child's World®: Mary Berendes, Publishing Director
The Design Lab: Design and production

Library of Congress Cataloging-in-Publication Data
Watson, S. B., 1953–
  Weird animal sports / by S.B. Watson.
      p. cm.
  Includes bibliographical references and index.
  ISBN 978-1-60954-375-4 (library bound: alk. paper)
  1. Sports—Juvenile literature. 2. Animals—Juvenile literature.
  3. Curiosities and wonders—Juvenile literature. I. Title.
  GV705.4.W37 2011
  796–dc22   2010042897

Photo credits:
Cover: AP/Wide World (top); iStock (bottom)
Interior: AP/Wide World: 13, 14, 18, 21; Corbis: 6; Kelly Ellifritz:
9; iStock: 5, 17; Catfish Sutton: 10; Huw Evans Photos: 22

Printed in the United States of America
Mankato, Minnesota
December, 2010
PA02070

*Above: In an ostrich race,
the feathers really fly!
See page 6 for more.*

*For more information
about the photo on
page 1, turn to page 20.*

TABLE OF CONTENTS

Get ready . . . get set . . . oink! Pigs can be seen racing at county fairs (page 16).

Can You Really Saddle a Hamster?

Animals are a big part of many people's lives. Some people enjoy having pets. Some love to ride horses. Others enjoy watching animals in the wild. And then there are weird sports involving animals! That's what we'll be looking at in this book. So grab your saddle, cheer on your frog, and watch out for that elephant's trunk. It's time for Weird Animal Sports!

Are these kids—and their dog—watching pig racing or elephant soccer?

FAST FACT!

The ostrich is the fastest land bird in the world. It can run at speeds up to 45 mph (72 km/h)!

Take a Two-Legged Trot

The **jockey** rides his animal forward. He feels another rider gaining on him. He rounds the track, and the finish line comes into view. Leaning forward, he tries to get extra speed. He crosses the finish line first . . . and pats his ostrich gently on the head. *Ostrich?* Yes, his ostrich! Ostrich racing has become popular in Africa as well as several places around the United States. The races are run on horse-racing tracks. Jockeys sit on the birds' strong backs. Ostriches can also pull a cart in which the driver sits.

Ostrich races are held in Africa, where ostriches make their homes.

Take a Flying Leap . . . or Two

The athletes line up at the start. Excitement mounts as everyone waits. And then . . . they're off! Or should we say, "They're up"? In the weird sport of frog jumping, frog owners yell, scream, and **encourage** their frogs to jump as far and as fast as they can. At some events, the frog that makes the single longest jump wins. At others, the frog that goes the farthest in a set amount of time is the winner. Frog wranglers are not allowed to touch their small **amphibian** athletes. They can only shout things like "You'll get extra flies tonight, Greeny. Come on!"

The most famous frog jumping event is in Calaveras County, California. Author Mark Twain wrote a famous story about a contest there.

RRIB-IT!

Did you know that National Frog-Jumping Day takes place each year on May 13?

SPLISH SPLASH!

Some noodlers have caught fish weighing as much as 60 pounds (27 kg)!

Noodling . . . and We Don't Mean Pasta!

Let's go fishing . . . with no rods, reels, hooks, or poles. The only gear you'll need is your own two hands. This type of fishing is called noodling. Noodlers catch fish, usually catfish, using only their bare hands. Absolutely no equipment or fishing gear is allowed. This slippery sport goes by many names, including grabbling, graveling, hogging, dogging, gurgling, tickling, and stumping. But be careful when you noodle—some of those catfish have sharp teeth!

If you go noodling, you'll be as wet as the fish you catch . . . with your bare hands!

Bowling With Dinner

Turkey bowling is the same as regular bowling, with one big difference—instead of rolling a bowling ball, players roll frozen turkeys! Also, instead of pins, bowlers aim at 10 plastic bottles. Okay, *two* big differences! Each player slides a frozen turkey down a smooth surface, trying to knock down the bottles. This weird sport began indoors. Bored shoppers slid frozen turkeys down grocery-store aisles!

Outdoor turkey bowling is usually played on frozen ponds or rivers.

GOBBLE GOBBLE!

Turkey bowling is used as a half-time event at some hockey games in the United States and Canada.

13

RACING TIP

Racing camels can reach speeds up to 25 mph (40 km/h) as they zoom around the track.

It's Humpy by a nose . . . and boy, that's a pretty big nose!

One Hump or Two?

Camel racing is like horse racing . . . but with camels. Jockeys on saddles ride camels around a track. The sport of camel racing has been around since the seventh century. Camel racing is popular in many countries, including India, Saudi Arabia, Egypt, Jordan, and Australia. One of the biggest annual events in the sport is the Camel Cup. This race is held in Alice Springs, Australia.

Pick a Pack of Pesky Porkers

Pig racing is a popular attraction at county fairs. The pigs don't have jockeys, however! Young pigs race around a small track made of dirt, grass, or gravel. In some versions, **obstacles** are placed along the way. Pigs must jump over gates—like a runner clearing high **hurdles**—or leap over bales of hay. In addition to many fairs, pig racing is also a regular event at baseball games for a Minnesota minor-league team.

The pigs wear scarves or small sweaters so that fans can follow their favorites around the track.

HAM IT UP!

The pigs are usually given silly names: Darth Oinker, Harry Porker, or Shakin' Bacon!

TINY TRIVIA!

The world record, shared by several hamsters, is 38 seconds to cover a track that is 30 feet (9 m) long.

The hamsters make the large blue wheels spin, which powers the "car" down the track.

Hamsters at High Speed!

Hamster racing rocks! In this weird sport, hamsters are put into hamster wheels or hamster balls. Then those wheels are attached to mini race cars. The cars take off down a track. The first critter to the finish wins! The hamsters have human helpers to make sure they keep on rolling. The sport became popular in England after a fear of disease cancelled the regular horse-racing schedule. In the United States, many pet stores sell hamster racing gear.

No Hands . . . Yes Trunks!

Today's World Cup soccer stars better watch out. They've got some competition from a three-ton (2,722 kg) opponent! In one type of elephant soccer, humans ride the animals. Two teams match up while riding the enormous beasts. In another type, humans play against riderless elephants. The animals can kick the soccer ball with all four legs. The elephants can pick the ball up with their trunks, flip it toward their hind legs, and kick it mid-air into the goal! It's probably best not to try to take the ball away from them!

These animals in Thailand were painted with different countries' flags for an Elephant World Cup!

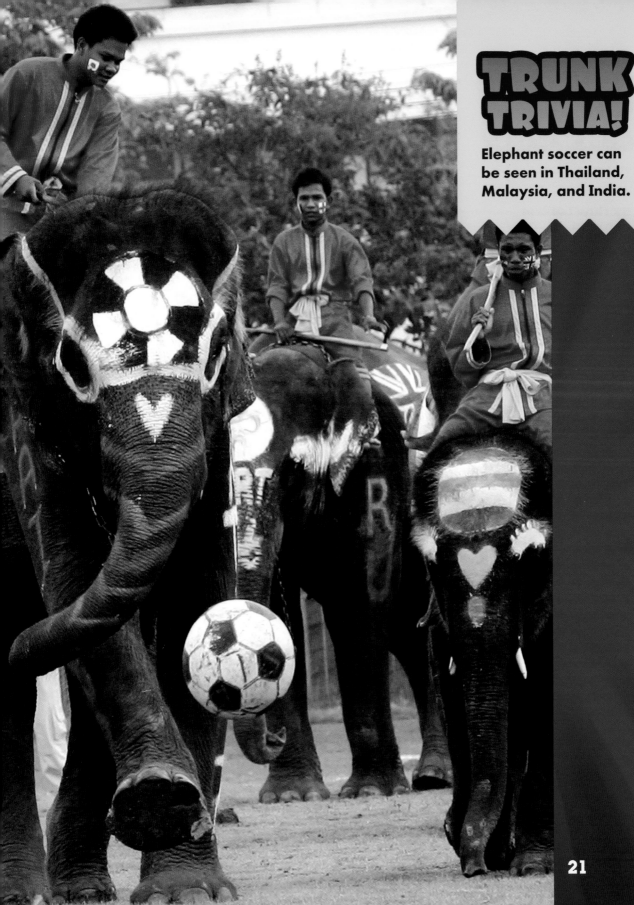

TRUNK TRIVIA!

Elephant soccer can be seen in Thailand, Malaysia, and India.

21

HORSIN' AROUND

The fastest time by a human was 2:05:19 by Huw Lobb in 2004. The fastest horse's time was 1:30 by a horse named Hussar, ridden by Zoe Jennings in 1991.

The man is ahead in this photo . . . but his four-legged opponent is gaining fast!

A Long-Distance Trot

The first runner starts, racing along a grassy track. He knows that the race is long and he must pace himself. Then the second runner takes off. This athlete has a rider sitting on its back! The first runner is human. The second is a horse. The two racers run a 22-mile (35-km) course. This race began in Llanwrtyd Wells, Wales, in 1980. Two men got into an argument. One man said that over a long distance a person could outrun a horse. The other disagreed, and so the race was on. In the years since, both people and horses have won the race!

Glossary

amphibian—animals that start their lives breathing water and end up breathing air.

encourage—to cheer or prod toward success

hurdles—a barrier; in racing, a small wooden gate that runners must jump over

jockey—the rider of an animal in a race

obstacles—barriers or anything blocking the way

Web Sites

For links to learn more about weird sports: **childsworld.com/links**

Note to Parents, Teachers, and Librarians: We routinely verify our Web links to make sure they are safe and active sites. So encourage your readers to check them out!

Index